CONTENTS

FOREWORD

Dear Friends:

It gives me great pleasure to pen the forward to this book, and not just because all the arrangements inside are songs I happened to write. The joy comes from my continuing association with the good name of Fred Bock.

Fred and I became fast friends when we first met each other in 1969. Not only did we share a love of music, but we soon discovered we both had the same odd hobby – collecting the funny names of real people. These poor souls had parents cruel enough to burden them with actual names like…

Farvel Fetz   Fusaye Ichinose

Eloise Snorf   Leslie Dogoldogol

Chester Gooser   Everredde McCrimnon

Finus Shellnut (My Favorite)   Abraham C. Gesundheit

Firmnin Swimnin   Fay Finfer

Crescenzo G. Fonzo   Lyman Flenner

Girley Logsdon Crum   Hartman Dingus

Fred often wondered aloud if people would still want to sing "He Touched Me" if it had been written by a guy named Finus Shellnut. I guess we'll never know…

My love and respect for Fred wasn't limited to his legendary sense of humor. Perhaps his finest quality was always aspiring to excellence - be it in his music, in his caring relationships with friends, or in his deep love for Lois and their two sons. Fred's motivation stemmed from his unwavering belief that God loves us, and that love demands our very best. Amen.

I think you'll discover Fred's commitment to excellence on every page of this book. Fred had this wonderful talent for arranging, which, when he was finished, made the song seem better than it was originally – especially mine!

I remember fondly the first time I heard Fred play his arrangement of "Let's Just Praise The Lord." In a few delicate phrases, Fred captured its true essence – the simple joy of worshiping our loving Father.

I miss Fred dearly, as I'm sure many of you do. But our good fortune is that Fred Bock will always be with us - every time we sit down at the piano.

Your friend,

Bill Gaither

Bill Gaither
Alexandria, Indiana
January, 2001

Let's Just Praise the Lord

William J. and Gloria Gaither
Arranged by Fred Bock

4

a little brighter

melody

(♫ = ♫) *a bit more rhythmic*

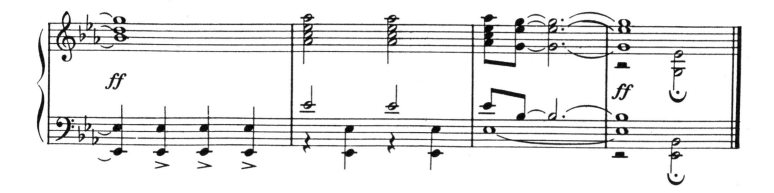

The King Is Coming

William J. and Gloria Gaither and Charles Millhuff
Arranged by Fred Bock

In a meditative style

Brightly, with a strong gospel feel

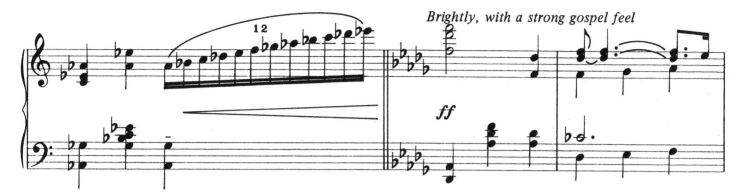

Get All Excited

William J. Gaither
Arranged by Fred Bock

Little louder

cresc.

Something Beautiful

William J. and Gloria Gaither
Arranged by Fred Bock

Warmly, with feeling

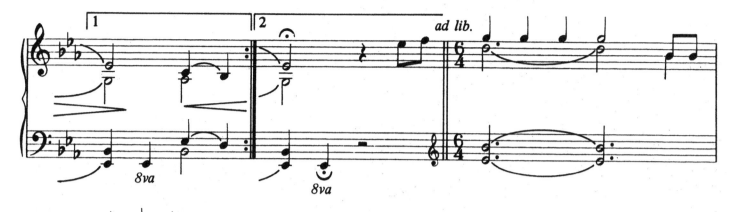

He Touched Me

William J. Gaither
Arranged by Fred Bock

He Started the Whole World Singing

William J. and Gloria Gaither and Chris Waters
Arranged by Fred Bock

Brightly

light shuffle, relaxed

The Church Triumphant

William J. and Gloria Gaither
Arranged by Fred Bock

a little faster

The Longer I Serve Him

William J. Gaither
Arranged by Fred Bock

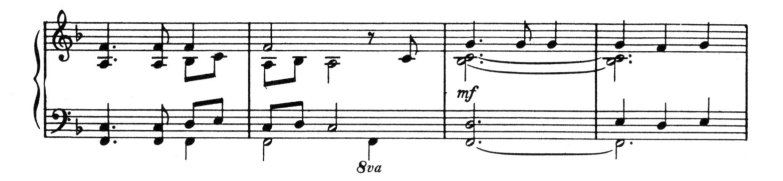

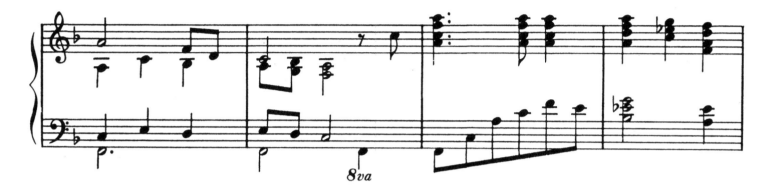

Old Friends

William J. and Gloria Gaither and J. D. Miller
Arranged by Fred Bock

In a relaxed, easy tempo (♩ =80)

 32

Even So, Lord Jesus, Come

William J. and Gloria Gaither
Arranged by Fred Bock

Good practice for crossing hands!

I Will Serve Thee

William J. and Gloria Gaither
Arranged by Fred Bock

Tenderly

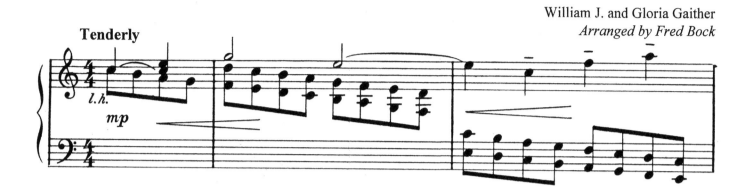

a little faster and smoother

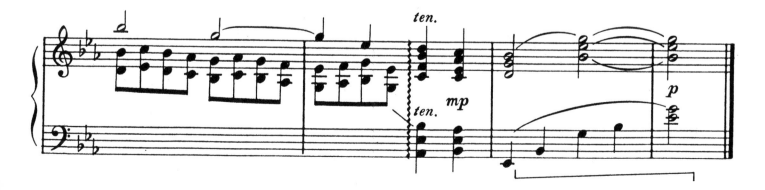

God Gave the Song

William J. and Gloria Gaither and Ronn Huff

Arranged by Fred Bock

Moderato, gently

gradually building